For all Nittany Lion cubs who will be nurtured in the spirit and traditions of Dear Old State.

For our family of Nittany Lions: Patrick, Gabby, Doug, and Rachel.

For all animal lovers, especially those who rescue, and for those who love their pets as much as their favorite team.

For Lockett, my inspiration, who longingly dreams of being a Nittany Lion like the rest of his family.

www.mascotbooks.com

Nittany and Me

For more information, please contact:
Mascot Books, an imprint of Amplify Publishing Group
620 Herndon Parkway #320
Herndon, VA 20170
info@mascotbooks.com

The indicia featured on this product is a protected trademark owned by Penn State University.

CPSIA Code: PRT1022A
ISBN-13: 978-1-64543-999-8

Printed in the United States

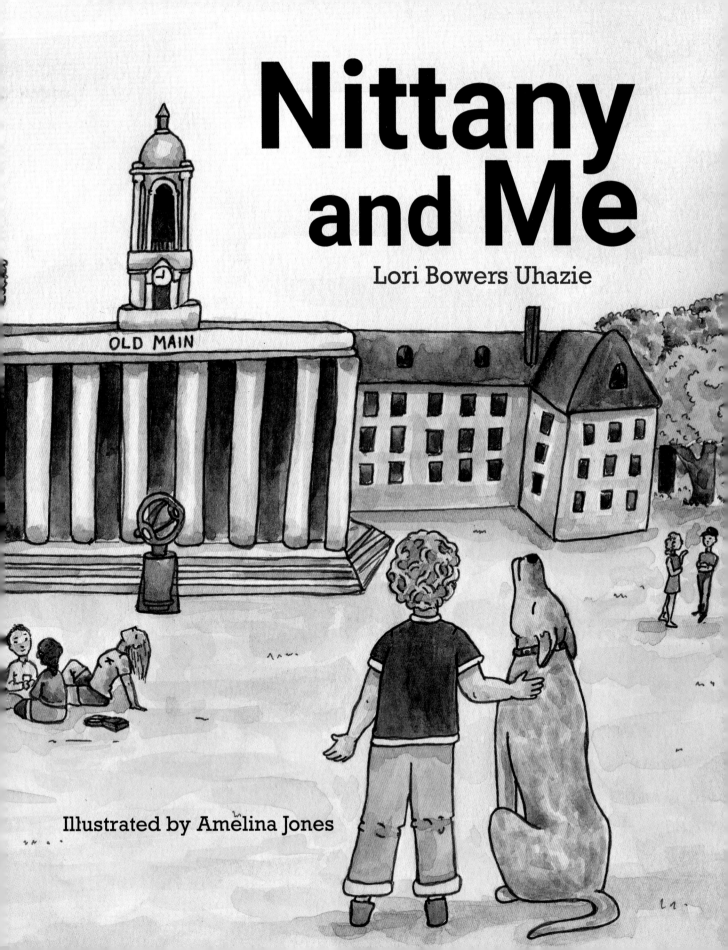

I love the mountains.
They're so much fun to run.
Nittany loves them too,
especially THIS one.

I love ice cream.
My favorite's blue and white.
Nittany loves it too.
We smile with every bite.

I love the dance marathon.
Its goal is a cure.
Nittany loves it too.
"For the Kids®" for sure!

I love the squirrels.
They're friendly on the mall.
Nittany loves them too,
THIS one most of all.

GO PENN STATE!

I love the lawn.
It's a great place to play.
Nittany loves it too.
Here, we learn "go" and "stay."

I love the bell.
Such sweet notes it sings.
Nittany loves it too.
He howls as it rings.

I love all sports.
Winter, spring, and fall.
Nittany loves them too.
He's great at volleyball.

I love the stadium.
At night it's extra loud.
Nittany loves it too,
wearing white and standing proud.

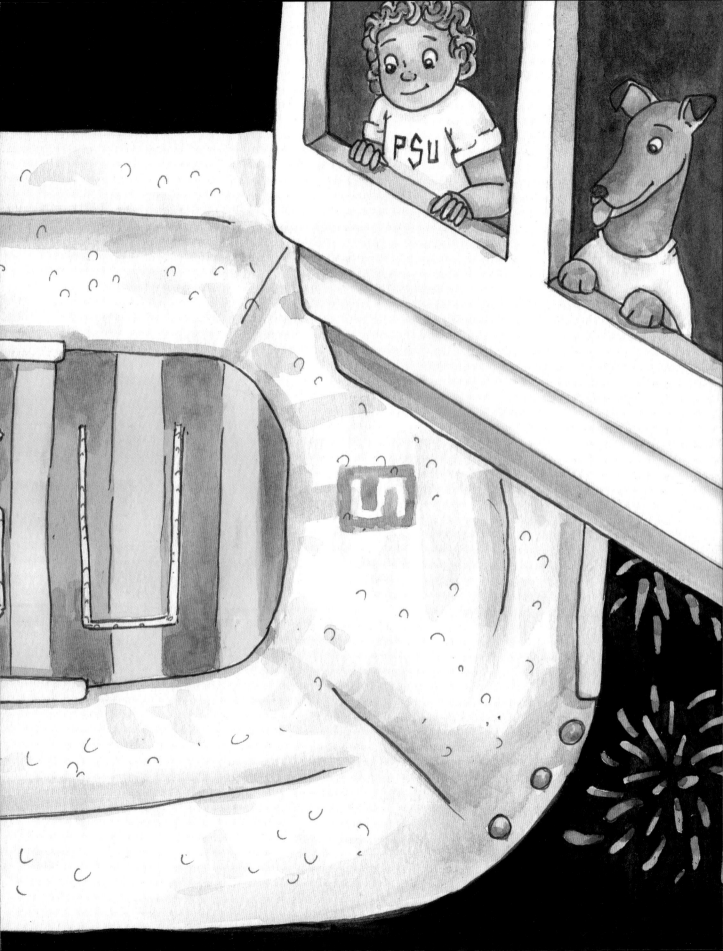

I love the S Zone.
It's above the team's gate.
Nittany loves it too.
We yell, "LET'S GO STATE!"

I love the lion.
He does push-ups galore.
Nittany loves him too.
We count with each score!

Nittany loves them too.
We can sing them all day.

I love the marching band.
Their high step is great.
Nittany loves them too.
We march in counts of eight.

I love the drum major.
They wear a very tall hat.
Nittany loves them too,
and wants to flip like that.

I love the twirlers.
Their batons fly through the air.
Nittany loves them too,
watching them catch with such flair.

I love the dance team.
They move so quick in beat.
Nittany loves them too,
and their high-flying feet.

I love the cheers.
I'm proud to shout, "WE ARE!"
Nittany loves them too.
He dreams that he's the star.

I love the lion shrine.
We always gather here.
Nittany loves it too.
We'll be back, year after year.

Nittany Lions Tips and Trivia

Mountains: Folklore and legends of the Nittany Valley revolve around a Native American Princess, Nita-Nee, for whom many believe the mountain was named. Penn State fans also refer to the area as "Happy Valley."

Practice saying "Nit-Nee."

Ice Cream: Berkey Creamery is famous for its "cow to cone," one size/one flavor only servings. Only one person ever received two flavors: President Bill Clinton. The Penn State-themed blue and white flavor is "Lion S'mores."

Find blue and white items on each page.

Dance Marathon: THON is the largest student-run fundraiser in the world. The 46-hour dance marathon benefits Four Diamonds for childhood cancer at Penn State Children's Hospital. Many millions of dollars have been raised, "For the Kids" (FTK®).

Try making a diamond shape with your fingers while shouting "FTK®!"

Squirrels: "Sneezy" is an actual squirrel on campus that photographer and Penn State alumna Mary Krupa dresses up for special occasions. You can follow this special little squirrel on Facebook at Sneezy the Penn State Squirrel or on Instagram at @sneezysquirrel. Read Sneezy's sign: "Go Penn State."

Lawn and Bell: Old Main, the office of Penn State's president, overlooks a large lawn, where students play and relax. The bell in the tower plays part of the school fight song, "Hail to the Lion," on Fridays and Saturdays.

Learn the words to "Hail to the Lion," which can be found on the inside of the front cover.

Sports: Penn State has one of the nation's biggest college athletic programs, featuring 31 varsity teams—16 mens and 15 womens.

Name the sport in each illustration. Which one is your favorite?

Stadium: Beaver Stadium has 106,572 seats, making it the second largest stadium in the US. Record attendance, however, was 110,889 fans at the 2018 Penn State White Out® game the Nittany Lions played vs. Ohio State. During the Penn State White Out, ALL fans wear white, creating what many say is the Greatest Show in College Sports.

What is the name of the stadium?

Football: Penn State football is known for its traditional uniforms. Players do not wear their names on their jerseys, and there are no logos or achievement stickers on their helmets. Instead, the team wears blue and white, plain and simple.

You're the quarterback! Find the receiver and the "PSU" sign.

S Zone: Lion Ambassadors, a spirited student group, form the "S" in the student section, located above the tunnel where the football team enters Beaver Stadium through the Penn State gate.

Trace the letter "S," and call out a cheer. S-T-A-T-E!

Lion: The Nittany Lion Mascot appears at university events all year long. He is best known for his trademark one-handed pushups. At football games, he does one for every point scored, and the crowd counts along, pumping their arm with each pushup.

Count to 7, the number of points for a touchdown and extra point.

Fight Songs: Two popular Penn State fight songs, "Hail to the Lion" and "Fight on State," are played during the marching band's famous "Floating LIONS" pregame drill, established in 1965.

Learn the words to each song found on the inside front and back covers. Find Penn State's original school colors, pink and black.

Marching Band: The Penn State Blue Band has about 320 members and they use high step style, 8 to 5 marching (8 steps per 5 yards).

Practice marching 8 counts, starting on the left foot.

Drum Major: The drum major leads the Blue Band onto the field and performs one of the most unique college marching band traditions: strutting through the band and doing a front flip with a tall hat on. Some believe if the drum major lands on their feet, Penn State will win the game.

Become a drum major for the day! Practice your best salute.

Twirlers: The featured baton twirler for the Blue Band is called the "Blue Sapphire," and the line of majorettes is called the "Touch of Blue."

Count the batons and strike a pose.

Dance Team: Called the "Lionettes," the Penn State dance team is famous for their kickline into a flying split.

Perform in the famous Lionette kickline!

Kick left, kick right. Repeat as often as you like. Don't forget to point your toes!

Cheers: As part of the Penn State Spirit Squad, cheerleaders lead one of the most famous cheers in college sports: "WE ARE…PENN STATE." That cheer represents a proud history of school spirit and unity.

Become an honorary part of the Penn State Spirit Squad! Call out "WE ARE!" and wait for a friend or caregiver to reply: "PENN STATE!" Repeat this cheer three times.

Lion Shrine: Sculpted in 1942, the lion shrine is the most photographed spot on campus. People line up for photos at the statue with their Penn State family. Piling on is welcomed, and all are encouraged to come and smile for the camera.

Say "NITTANY" with a big SMILE!

About the Author

Lori Bowers Uhazie is a Penn State alumna ('82 Comm), who experienced many of Penn State's gameday traditions up close and personal as the "Blue Sapphire" (featured baton twirler) of the Blue Band. She lives in Rochester, New York, with her husband, David ('82), whom she met in the Blue Band. They raised two Nittany Lion cubs, Patrick Steven, a.k.a. PSU ('13) and Doug ('17), who are also Blue Band alums. The family remains active in many Penn State organizations.

Lori enjoys golfing, hiking, and traveling, and is the proud PawMa to a rescued and retired champion greyhound, @lockett.the.rocket.